G000167619

Beside Still Waters

BESIDE STILL WATERS
Favorite Prayers, Poems, and Scriptures to Calm the Soul

Cover image: Evgeniya Gaydarova/iStock
Cover design: Lauren Williamson

Print ISBN: 978-1-5064-5910-3

Favorite Prayers, Poems, and
Scriptures to Calm the Soul

BESIDE
still
WATERS

ANGELA PALFREY

Augsburg Books

MINNEAPOLIS

contents

Love

Love is patient and kind:
it is not jealous or conceited or proud;
Love is not ill-mannered
or selfish or irritable;
Love does not keep a record of wrongs;
Love is not happy with evil,
but is happy with the truth.
Love never gives up;
and its faith, hope, and patience
never fail.

1 Corinthians 13:4-7

The Gate of the Year

I said to the man who stood at
the gate of the year, "Give me a
light that I may tread safely
into the unknown." And he
replied—"Go out into the
darkness and put your hand
into the hand of God.
That shall be to you better than light
and safer than a known way!"

So I went forth and finding the
hand of God, trod gladly into
the night. And he led me
toward the hills and the
breaking of day in the lone East.

Minnie Louise Haskins

Prayer of Francis of Assisi

Lord, make me
an instrument of your peace:
where there is hatred, let me sow love:
where there is injury, pardon:
where there is doubt, faith:
where there is darkness, light:
where there is despair, hope,
and where there is sadness, joy.

Divine Master, grant that
I may not so much seek
to be consoled as to console,
to be understood as to understand,
to be loved as to love.

For it is in giving that we receive,
it is in pardoning that we
are pardoned,
and in dying that we are
born to eternal life.

A Prayer for Those Who Live Alone

I live alone, dear Lord, stay by my side;
in all my daily needs be thou my guide.
Grant me good health, for that indeed I pray,
to carry on my work from day to day.

Keep pure my mind, my thoughts, my every deed,
let me be kind, unselfish, in my neighbor's need.

Spare me from fire, from flood, malicious tongues,
from thieves, from fear, and evil ones.

If sickness or an accident befall,
then humbly, Lord, I pray, hear thou my call.
And when I'm feeling low, or in despair,
lift up my heart and help me in my prayer.
I live alone, dear Lord, yet have no fear,
because I feel your presence ever near.

Amen

I Said a Prayer...

I said a prayer for you today
and know God must have heard—
I felt the answer in my heart
although he spoke no word!
I didn't ask for wealth or fame
(I knew you wouldn't mind)—
I asked him to send treasures
of a far more lasting kind!

I asked that he'd be near you
at the start of each new day
to grant you health and blessings
and friends to share your way!
I asked for happiness for you
in all things great and small—
but it was for his loving care
I prayed the most of all!

"God Bless You"

How sweetly fall those simple words
upon the human heart;
when friends in holiest terms thus seek
their best wish to impart.
From far or near, they ever seem
to bear a power to cheer you;
and soul responsive beats to soul
in breathing out:
"God bless you."

The Beatitudes

Blessed are the poor in spirit,
for theirs is the kingdom of heaven.

Blessed are those who mourn,
for they shall be comforted.

Blessed are the meek,
for they shall inherit the earth.

Blessed are those who hunger
and thirst for righteousness,
for they shall be satisfied.

Blessed are the merciful,
for they shall obtain mercy.

Blessed are the pure in heart,
for they shall see God.

Blessed are the peacemakers,
for they shall be called sons of God.

Blessed are those who are persecuted
for righteousness' sake,
for theirs is the kingdom of heaven.

Matthew 5:3-10

Deep Peace . . .

Deep peace of the Running Wave to you.
Deep peace of the Flowing Air to you.
Deep peace of the Quiet Earth to you.
Deep peace of the Shining Stars to you.
Deep peace of the Son of Peace to you.

Celtic Benediction

Friendship

A friend is like a tower strong;
a friend is like the joyous song
that helps us on our way.
When golden ties of friendship bind
the heart to heart, the mind to mind,
how fortunate are we!

For friendship is a noble thing;
it soars past death on angel's wing
into eternity.
God blesses friendship's holy bond
both here and in the great beyond:
a benefit unpriced.

Then may we know that wondrous joy,
that precious ore without alloy;
a friendship based on Christ.

Death Is Nothing At All

Death is nothing at all.
I have only slipped away
into the next room.

I am I, and you are you.
Whatever we were to each other,
that we still are.

Call me by my old familiar name,
speak to me in the easy way
which you always used.

Put no difference in your tone,
wear no forced air of solemnity or sorrow.
Laugh as we always laughed
at the little jokes we
enjoyed together.

Let my name be ever
the household word
that it always was,
let it be spoken without effect,
without the trace of a shadow on it.

Life means all that it ever meant.
It is the same as it ever was;
there is unbroken continuity.

Why should I be out of mind
because I am out of sight?

I am waiting for you,
for an interval,
somewhere very near,
just around the corner.

All is well.

Henry Scott Holland

What Is Dying?

A ship sails and I stand
watching till she fades
on the horizon and someone
at my side says, "She is gone."
Gone where?
Gone from my sight,
that is all;
she is just as large
as when I saw her.
The diminished size and
total loss of sight is in me,
not in her, and just at the moment
when someone at my side says,
"She is gone,"
there are others who
are watching her coming
and other voices
take up a glad shout,
"There she comes!"
and that is dying.

Do Not Be Afraid

Do not be afraid, for I have redeemed you.
I have called you by your name; you are mine.

When you walk through the waters, I'll be with you;
you will never sink beneath the waves.

When the fear of loneliness is looming,
then remember I am at your side.

You are mine, O my child, I am your Father,
and I love you with a perfect love.

Based on Isaiah 43:1-5

A Blessing

May the Lord bless you
and take care of you;

May the Lord be kind
and gracious to you;

May the Lord look on you with favor
and give you peace.

Numbers 6:22-27

When Dreams are Broken

When dreams are broken things
and joy has fled,
there is Jesus.

When hope is a struggle
and faith a fragile thread,
there is Jesus.

When grief is a shadow
and peace unknown,
there is Jesus.

When we need the assurance
that we're not alone,
there is Jesus.

The Twenty-Third Psalm

The Lord is my shepherd,
I shall not want.

He makes me lie down
in green pastures.
He leads me beside still waters;
he restores my soul.

He guides me
in paths of righteousness
for his name's sake.

Even though I walk through
the valley of the
shadow of death,
I fear no evil;

for you are with me;
your rod and
your staff comfort me.

You prepare a table before me
in the presence of my enemies.
You anoint my head with oil.
My cup overflows.

Surely goodness and love
shall follow me
all the days of my life.
And I shall live
in the house of the Lord forever.

Prayer of Richard of Chichester

Thanks be to you,
my Lord Jesus Christ,
for all the benefits that
you have given me;
for all the pains and insults
that you have borne for me,
O most merciful Redeemer,
Friend, and Brother.
May I know you more clearly,
love you more dearly,
and follow you more nearly.

Kitchen Prayer

Lord of pots and pans and things,
since I've not time to be
a saint by doing lovely things,
or watching late with thee,
or dreaming in the dawn light,
or storming heaven's gates,
make me a saint by getting meals
and washing up the plates.

Although I must have Martha's hands,
I have a Mary mind,
and when I black the boots and shoes,
thy sandals, Lord, I find.
I think of how they trod the earth,
what time I scrub the floor;
accept this meditation, Lord,
I haven't time for more.

Footprints

One night I had a dream.
I dreamed I was walking along
the beach with
God, and across the sky flashed
scenes from my life. For each scene
I noticed two sets of footprints in
the sand, one belonged to me and
the other to God.

When the last scene of my life
flashed before me I looked back at
the footprints in the sand. I noticed
that at times along the path of life
there was only one set of footprints.

I also noticed that it happened at
the very lowest and saddest times
of my life. This really bothered me
and I questioned God about it.

"God, you said that once I decided to follow you, you would walk with me all the way, but I noticed that during the most troublesome times in my life there is only one set of footprints. I don't understand why in times when I needed you most, you would leave me."

God replied, "My precious, precious child, I love you and I would never, never leave you during your times of trials and suffering. When you see only one set of footprints it was then that I carried you."

Our Father

Our Father, who art in heaven,
hallowed be thy name.
Thy Kingdom come, thy will be done,
on earth as it is in heaven.

Give us this day our daily bread;
and forgive us our trespasses,
as we forgive those who trespass against us.

And lead us not into temptation,
but deliver us from evil.

For thine is the Kingdom,
the Power, and the Glory,
forever and ever.

Amen

Take Courage!

I can't change what you're going through,
I have no words to make a difference;
no answers or solutions
to make things easier for you.

But if it helps in any way,
I want to say I care.

Please know that even when you're lonely,
you're not alone.

I'll be here,
supporting you with all my thoughts,
cheering for you with all my strength,
praying for you with all my heart.

For whatever you need,
for as long as it takes—

Lean on my love.

The Power
of Prayer

The day was long, the burden I had
borne seemed heavier than I could
longer bear, and then it lifted—
but I did not know someone had knelt
in prayer; had taken me to God that
very hour, and asked the easing of
the load, and he, in infinite
compassion, had stooped down
and taken it from me.

We cannot tell how often as we
pray for some bewildered one, hurt
and distressed, the answer comes,
but many times those hearts find
sudden peace and rest.
Someone had prayed, and faith,
a reaching hand, took hold of God
and brought him down that day!
So many, many hearts
have need of prayer:
Oh, let us pray!

A Promise of Hope

I alone know the plans I have for you,
plans to bring you prosperity and not disaster,
plans to bring about the future you hope for.

Then you will call to me.

You will come and pray to me,
and I will answer you.

You will seek me,
and you will find me
because you will seek me
with all your heart.

Jeremiah 29:11-13

The Peace of God

Have no anxiety about anything
but in everything,
by prayer and supplication,
with thanksgiving, let your requests
be made known to God.

And the peace of God,
which passes all understanding,
will keep your hearts and your minds
in Christ Jesus.

Philippians 4:4-7

Take Time

Take time to THINK . . .
it is the source of power.

Take time to PLAY . . .
it is the secret of perpetual youth.

Take time to READ . . .
it is the fountain of wisdom.

Take time to PRAY . . .
it is the greatest power on earth.

Take time to LOVE and BE LOVED . . .
it is a God-given privilege.

Take time to **BE FRIENDLY** . . .
it is the road to happiness.

Take time to **LAUGH** . . .
it is the music of the soul.

Take time to **GIVE** . . .
it is too short a day to be selfish.

Take time to **WORK** . . .
it is the price of success.

Take time to **DO CHARITY** . . .
it is the key to heaven.

God's Promises

God has not promised
sun without rain,
joy without sorrow,
peace without pain.

But God has promised
strength for the day,
rest from the labor,
light for the way,
grace for the trials,
help from above,
unfailing sympathy,
undying love.

Hold My Hand

Hold my hand, Lord.
Walk me through the loneliness
and the valley of my sorrow.
Hold onto me when I'm afraid
to think about tomorrow.

Let me lean on you, Lord,
when I'm too weary to go on.

Hold my hand, Lord, through the night
until I see the light of dawn.

When You're Lonely

When you're lonely,
I wish you love.

When you're down,
I wish you joy.

When you're troubled,
I wish you peace.

When things are complicated,
I wish you simple beauty.

When things look empty,
I wish you hope.

The Divine Weaver

My life is but a weaving
between my Lord and me;
I cannot choose the colors
he worketh steadily.

Oftentimes he weaveth sorrow
and I, in foolish pride,
forget that he seeth the upper,
and I the under side.

Not till the loom is silent
and the shuttles cease to fly,
shall God unroll the canvas
and explain the reason why.

The dark threads are as needful
in the weaver's skillful hand
as the threads of gold and silver
in the pattern he has planned.

The Difference

I got up early one morning and
rushed right into the day;
I had so much to accomplish
that I didn't have time to pray.
Problems just tumbled about me,
and heavier came each task.
"Why doesn't God help me?"
I wondered;
he answered, "You didn't ask."

I wanted to see joy and beauty,
but the day toiled on gray
and bleak;

I wondered why God didn't show me;
he said, "You didn't seek."

I tried to come into God's presence;
I used all my keys at the lock.

God gently and lovingly chided,
"My child, you didn't knock."

I woke early this morning,
and paused before entering the day;
I had so much to accomplish
that I had to take time to pray.

One Solitary Life

He was born in an obscure village,
the child of a peasant woman.

He grew up in still another village
where he worked in a carpenter's
shop until he was thirty.

He did none of the things one
usually associates with greatness.

He had no credentials but himself.

He was only thirty-three when
public opinion turned against him.

He was turned over to his enemies
and was crucified.

When he was dead he was laid
in a borrowed grave.

Twenty centuries have passed
and today he is the central figure of
the human race.

No one has affected the life of man
on earth as much as that
ONE SOLITARY LIFE.

Prayer for Serenity

God grant me the SERENITY
to accept the things
I cannot change,

COURAGE to change
the things I can,

and WISDOM to know
the difference.

The Lord
Our Protector

I lift up my eyes to the hills.
From whence does my help come?
My help comes from the Lord,
who made heaven and earth.

He will not let your foot be moved,
he who keeps you will not slumber.
Behold, he who keeps Israel
will neither slumber nor sleep.

The Lord is your keeper;
the Lord is your shade on your right hand.
The sun shall not smite you by day,
nor the moon by night.

The Lord will keep you from all evil;
he will keep your life.

The Lord will keep your going out
and your coming in,
from this time forth,
and forevermore.

Psalm 121

The Cross in My Pocket

I carry a cross in my pocket;
a simple reminder to me
of the fact that I am a Christian
no matter where I may be.
This little cross is not magic,
nor is it a good-luck charm.
It isn't meant to protect me
from every physical harm.
It's not for identification
for all the world to see.
It's simply an understanding
between my Savior and me.
When I put my hand in my pocket

to bring out a coin or a key,
the cross is there to remind me
of the price he paid for me.
It reminds me, too, to be thankful
for my blessings day by day,
and to strive to serve him better
in all that I do and say.
It's also a daily reminder
of the peace and comfort I share
with all who know my Master
and give themselves to his care.
So, I carry a cross in my pocket
reminding no one but me
that Jesus Christ is the Lord of my life,
if only I'll let him be.

Sympathy

God be with you in your sorrow,
through the night and through the day;
may some blessing come tomorrow that
will clear its cloud away.

God is generous in his giving,
give him now the soul that's fled:
may he bless with
strength the living,
rest eternally the dead.

I Asked Jesus

I asked
JESUS,
"How much do
you love me?"
"This much,"
he answered, and
he stretched out
his arms and died.

Be Still

Be still, and know that I am God.

Psalm 46:10

Everything Is Possible

This is impossible
for a human being,
but for God
everything is possible.

Matthew 19:26

I Am with You Always

I am with you in the springtime
of your life, when joy is new,
and when the summer brings
the fullness of your faith,
I'm there with you.
I am with you in the autumn
of your years, to turn to gold
every memory of your yesterdays,
to banish winter's cold.
I am with you in the sunshine,
when your world glows warm and bright.
I am with you when life's shadows
bring long hours of endless night.
I am with you every moment,
every hour of every day—
Go in peace upon life's journey,
for I'm with you all the way.

Life's Journey

The road of life may take us
where we do not care to go;
up rocky paths, down darkened trails,
our steps unsure and slow.

But our dear Lord extends
his hands to hold, to help, to guide us;
we never have to feel alone
for he walks close beside us.

Prayer of Dedication

Lord Jesus,
I give my hands to do your work.
I give you my feet to go your way.
I give you my eyes to see as you do.
I give you my tongue to speak your words.
I give you my mind
that you may think in me.
I give you my spirit
that you may pray in me.
Above all, I give you my heart
that you may love in me.
I give you my whole self
that you may grow in me,
so that it is you,
Lord Jesus, who lives
and works
and prays in me.

Why?

Wisdom is not knowing all
the answers to the problems of each day.
Not knowing why this has happened
to me and not to someone else.
Not soaking up all the knowledge
this world can offer, but knowing
that behind the whole of life,
for now and evermore,
God is sovereign and,
though I may not understand,
he is working to make us
each according to his plan.

If we ask, there is an answer
to each problem,
though it may not be the one
we want to hear.
Believe your God will take
your hand if you allow.
Let him guide your every step,
and when you feel unsure
believe that he knows best.

Paul's Farewell

Be happy
and grow in Christ.

Do what I have said,
and live in harmony and peace.

May the grace
of our Lord Jesus Christ
be with you all.

May God's love, and
the Holy Spirit's Friendship,
be yours.

2 Corinthians 13:11-14